The Psychology of the Human-natural Heart

(April 2017)

*

Traumear

If psychology is ever to become anything other than a modern self-projection it will be practiced in order to draw attention to the split between reaction and reflection, to identify it as human-natural and positive while pointing in the direction of true creativity, so that contemporary souls may replace the modern psyche.

from: 'christianity', a book by the author

*

Psychology has the task, and is the task, of unfolding the psyche; it is the process of interpreting psychic phenomena in such a way that soul results.

from: '210 Apophthegms', a book by the author

*

The psychology of the human-natural heart, implies a wish to understand what it means to do good, to be communally creative, from the point of view of psyche. (pg. 5)

*

If by psychology we mean knowledge and understanding of the human psyche specifically for the purpose of translating psychic phenomena into operational soul, then we are justified in asking others to entrust us with their inward anxieties and lethargies. (pg. 51)

*

The Psychology of the Human-natural Heart

We need to know what happens to us when we are under duress. Often we need help in order to acquaint ourselves, from outside, as it were, with the various ways in which we are able to be trustworthy and to think honourably to the accompaniment of noble feeling.

Indeed a sense of honour is crucial for the human heart, since the heart is commonly seen as both seat and source of mood, temperament and emotion. At the same time we may choose to behave with a degree of nobility, finally in the interest of our peaceful progression through the difficulties and out of the problematic states of our existence.

Our problems and difficulties, in relation to honourable and noble feeling and thought, are psychic, which is to say that they amount to our resistance, initially reactive, to new life. We are responsible for the operations of our soul, which is to say: it is up to us to take responsibility for the cooperative behaviour of our soul and not to get caught up in psychic difficulties and diseases, as if we did not know the difference between psyche and soul.

So when we speak of the psychology of the human heart, what we mean is a sufficient understanding – sufficient to our personal needs – of the role played by our soul and of its reaction as psyche. Problems and difficulties arise when our soul registers new life on the horizon and draws it to our attention but we are not ready to receive and to perceive. Of course we cannot be one hundred percent ready for new life, that stands to reason. Whatever is new surprises us and new life is bound to surprise us completely. Our readiness, therefore, will reside in our willingness to cope intelligently and gladly with setbacks as being intrinsically apparent, not real. These set-backs include everything we generally mean by falsehood, evil and ugliness.

*

The clearest indication we can have of our soul is that we cannot think of what to do while we feel the compulsion to do. This lets us know that our soul, which is always desirous of being active, is being prevented by a mistaken attitude we have of creative spirit. Our heart is creative spirit. No myth is involved here. So perhaps we need to review what we know of creative spirit and how we understand it in relation to our being as human persons in community.

A workable definition of creative spirit might simply be the way in which merciful good spirit energizes our intention to do good in one way or another. The intention to do good arises with certainty from our human nature, where we are at liberty to wish, to desire, to crave and so on. When we wish to do good, then, for example, good spirit supplies us with the wherewithal to realize our wish. If for some silly reason we should wish to harm someone, it does not. Certainly it is always up to us in person whether we wish to do good or, for example, to harm someone, so how we make up our mind, this determines whether creative spirit is available to us and how much of it.

So there is our human nature, or the resurrected Jesus, if you prefer to think of it in that way, and then there is merciful good spirit, or god, while we, in symbolic relevance, find ourselves habituated in sovereign manner between the two.

(I should mention here that of course the modern spirit does not allow for an equation of our human nature with the resurrected Jesus. There are those who consider that it shames their human nature and others who will argue that it sullies their image of Jesus. Nonetheless, since we do not intend to be modern, we equate our human nature with the resurrected Jesus.)

A small point: If we *want* to do good, we either have something in mind that we consider to be good and this blocks the creative energy we need to do anything at all, or else we feel a vague sense of emptiness, we 'have a want', in which case we do well to refer this feeling to our human nature and to god as soon as possible because any indulgence in such a 'want' is just another sensual pleasure and in this case specifically a morbid one. Similarly if we suppose that sensual pleasure is good, we likewise distance ourselves from good spirit. In both cases, we might say, the fact that we want one thing or another should first be looked at in the light of contemporary (not modern) usefulness and expediency and the same for a feeling of 'want'.

In fact it is this 'want' to do good which first informs us of the difference between merciful good spirit and the modern spirit as creative energy. Modern spirit forever persuades us that we want this or that or the other. This spirit presents us with an image of ourselves as in one way or another being in want, to begin with either merely wanting, which is a kind of morbid tension, or 'in want' of some object or commodity or such. It does not first inform us of a lack in ourselves plain and simple so that we are free to decide pro or con but it right away tells us what it is we 'want'. It holds out to us a desirable object or state or circumstance in such a way that we want it and must have it and cannot do without it. The modern spirit is a great advertising agency and it knows how to operate subliminally. It insists that we take its word for the fact that we need this thing and cannot do without that thing and if we were to try to do without it we would only do violence to our precious sense of self and to our image of self – which image of course is initially instilled in us by the modern spirit. (We advisedly speak of *the* modern spirit but of good spirit.)

Creative spirit does not work like that. It merely lets us know that we are in need, or that we have a lack, or that we cannot cope. It leaves it to us freely to decide whether we will respond and how we will respond. If we are smart we will undertake to respond and to do so in terms of good spirit. The wish or the desire to do good, by which we will mean the intention to cooperate with good spirit in some work, depends on us.

So we can certainly try to understand as well as possible this difference between the modern spirit and good spirit, so that we will be less inclined to fall in with the former and more determined to cooperate with the latter. Understandably this takes discipline and practice.

Some knowledge of the difference between reaction and response can be sensibly reviewed now and again. When we react, whether we do it consciously or unconsciously, we signal that we want nothing to do with whatever is strange to us and threatening to change us. Knowledge is missing when we react unconsciously but understanding, plus knowledge of course, are missing when we react consciously. When some part of me reacts, such as when I blink or flinch, this is somewhat different from when I as an individual or I in person react. What is important for us to understand is that we are to be changed but we cannot be changed while we are expecting it. So all knowledge or reality has to start with those initial reactions – to which we do well then to respond, in the sense that we, as it were, switch on our god-given awareness and allow it full scope. Shall we say that philosophy proper starts with reactions to the unknown and actual science begins with reactions to reactions to the unknown? – Here is plenty of room for further enquiry along that line.

*

Our topic, the psychology of the human-natural heart, implies a wish to understand what it means to do good, to be communally creative, from the point of view of psyche.

I refrain especially from saying '*the* psyche', because once someone is committed to psychic 'being' and behaviour, god alone can help him because human wisdom alone is powerless. Whatever we do creatively from our own initiative does of course imply our cooperation with good spirit, but it also means that if someone is to draw benefit from our work he is bound, to a degree, to become dissatisfied with his psychic existence. This dissatisfaction, in whatever shape or form it turns up within him, is indirectly due to the interest good spirit takes in him, and he, of course, is now at liberty to ignore or even to resist this interest to the extent of his dissatisfaction. Naturally any interest god takes in us is to be welcomed with open arms, not rejected in the way we would do if we concentrated on dealing with this psychic phenomenon, our dissatisfaction, in ignorance of good spirit.

To the extent of our actual commitment to psyche, we have no soul and are not open to the input of good spirit. Soul, therefore, is beneficially seen as our cooperative being with god, which takes psychic beings, or phenomena, into account, cleverly, as raw-materials. If we were to define a modern human being from this angle we might say that one moment he is trapped in psychic behaviour and apparently satisfied, and the next moment he is really dissatisfied and at liberty from psychic behaviour. The difference between liberty and freedom escapes him as much as the difference between soul and psyche. We can certainly try to help him out of this impasse but only if he has come to the end of his modern tether and wants to be helped.

Now contemporary psychology is knowledge for the sake of understanding psyche. It is fundamentally a search for the wisdom that will allow us, specifically, to step out of our modern time-zone into contemporary existence towards eternal life here and now. As we forge ahead, we do not see ourselves as scientists, which is to say as specialists in some terminologically closed-off corner of materialist or spiritualist research-activity, but rather as human beings who rely on our compassion to familiarize ourselves with the predicaments and afflictions of those who are perhaps even worse off than we are and so we shoulder one or two of their burdens for the time it takes to render them bearable. So in the present case we can see how our fellow man may be struggling and essentially in two mutually contradictory minds as to what contribution he can make both to his own wellbeing and to the wellbeing of others. His creativity is paralyzed. His understanding of himself either ends in hopelessness or in ignorance. He has either too much or too little energy and his achievements leave him fundamentally dissatisfied. For one example, he produces wonders of technical sophistication and then his adolescent illusion of immortality burns out. For the remainder of his existence he clings to the shell of this existential reproduction of himself and fights tooth and nail for 'public funding'. [1]

How readily we are willing to condemn those who lack our advantages, until we recall that none of our achievements are really due to independent, egotistic effort. Whatever we have truly created, which therefore has lasting value, has been initiated within us by good spirit, while our own initiative, no doubt praiseworthy, came afterwards, in response. While it makes sense that we should be proud of those responses, at the same time we feel inclined to humility while we keep in mind that strictly in terms of our individual selves we can do nothing.

So we can see how in our modernity we vacillate between arrogance and timidity, while as contemporary human beings we are proud and humble at the same time.

* *

Our human-natural heart, as the seat of creative spirit, allows us, for example, to identify the generic drive as a fundamental constituent. We are 'driven' in the direction of manhood or womanhood. How we cooperate with this drive determines whether we arrive or not. Initially, of course, we react to every instance of it. We are bound to

---

[1] 'Public funding' in terms of money, prestige or popular applause.

7

experience it each time as an unfamiliar change and therefore as a threat. This is not merely some part of us reacting, such as when our eye blinks or some muscle causes us to flinch, but it is we ourselves in person who draw back.

All our initial reactions are unintentional but not all are personal. So we might say that the generic drive actually draws our attention to whether we exist only as individuals or more, as individual persons. As individuals we are at the beck and call of our 'drives' but as persons we tend to think at least a little about what moves us and about whether or not we want to be moved – or should we maybe hold still? As a matter of fact, as individuals we cannot make out the generic drive as such and find ourselves urged more or less forcefully to take issue, if we might, first of all with our lack or personal being. We find ourselves urged alright but this does not mean that we will automatically try to face up to that urge. If we decide to persevere as individuals, perhaps even as individualists, such urges are simply a nuisance and perhaps treated with medication or interpreted out of the way. Maybe we become obese.[1] As individuals, after all, we want our comforts and conveniences, we want to be left in peace to vegetate. So let's face it, we will not wish to hear about 'the human-natural heart' in the first place.

We may begin therefore, we human persons, with that peculiar phenomenon which heralds an onset of the generic drive and which occurs to us as a phenomenon rather than as a being, because we have reacted. As a consequence of our reaction we are faced with something we cannot readily identify. We become more and more tense.

---

[1] Psychically or corporeally obese. (L. lit. 'that which has devoured'; Skeat)

(I myself these days become very itchy too, as soon as that drive addresses me.)

So we become tense – let's stick with that description for the moment – and we fish around for what might be causing the tension. If I were modern, I would right away 'know' that I have to 'have sex'. I would not speak of a mysterious tension which I would eventually identify accurately as an onset of the generic drive but I would right away 'know', in my modern, uncontemporary way, that I need to satisfy this sex-drive. I have to have sex or I will get no peace. If I am married, I will try to persuade my wife (my husband?) to have sex with me, which I might also call 'making love'. Of course I would be quite capable of 'making love', as I would call it, whether I was married or not.

I should maybe remind here, that the generic drive is good-spiritual, not carnal, and that my cooperation is required if it is to achieve its end, namely my mature manhood. A modern male individual mistakes it for a carnal thing, specifically for 'the sex drive', so he will want rid of it. If he can gain some gratuitous pleasure during the process, so much the better. As a modern individualist he might even get into the more or less addictive bad habit of bringing on the sex drive, for the pleasure of getting rid of it again (pornography). What can you say. Perhaps he is reacting to some socio-religious, moralistic ideology that strives to turn him into a good person and he won't have that. We can understand that. We can none of us be good persons and the sooner we find that out the better.

What we can be is mature men and women in the sight of god and if that is our ambition we will strive to replace our modernity with something better. We will sooner rather than later recognize that peculiar tension that is nearly driving us round the bend as psychic and as an onset of the generic drive. Quickly the annoyance will give place to reconsideration and then to gratitude. Why gratitude? Because we are seriously eager to become more mature men and women and to continue to behave and act maturely.

*

Psychic tension, then, indicates the generic drive from one side as it initially draws our attention. And since we have defined it in terms of our reaction to it, depending on our state of being at the time, and since every such reaction is fundamentally a physical rejection of something, all we have to ask is, would we be smarter to do the opposite, namely accept what is coming our way. We definitely would like the generic substance to be imparted to us, for the simple reason that to do so is in our interest as human beings; human beings want to be creative as they grow towards maturity and in maturity; in other words as they develop and evolve.

Right away we recall to mind that the tension we understand as an unintentional reaction to gender is only one side of the coin, the other side being an extreme lethargy. It is of a very peculiar kind. We almost desire to persist in it. This is most strange. Ordinary lethargy is more like a hateful weariness accompanied perhaps by nausea but mostly it amounts to an unwillingness to do anything plus a feeling that we could not do anything if we tried plus the notion that nothing is really worth doing. All that and sometimes more, depending on our constitution. The lethargy due to our reaction to gender however would seem to amount to a shut-down of the reasoning faculty, while at the same time we could swear that if we were just to give in to whatever this is, we would never want to – or be able to – escape from it. The only thing that works for us now is that we force our self out of the way by acting energetically, outwardly, perhaps angrily, even violently. It is our self, indeed, that has us in its grip and promises us eternal life if we just protect it against this energetic generic substance which is, indeed, threatening to wipe it out. The foretaste of the eternal life it promises is the lethargy I have been describing. How horrible! we say and may be we even shout it as we give ourselves a violent shake in order to return to our reasonable senses and consequently to our sense of human being.

So these two things are what our human-natural heart has to cope with when the chips are down, especially during our evolutionary growth, when our main interest is not our own development but the development of those for whom we make ourselves responsible.

The lethargy, again, compares to what we might experience on Mt. Everest when we run short of oxygen. There is an undeniable temptation to lie down and give ourselves over to forgetfulness and death. The tension, by comparison, is more like a surfeit of oxygen, when we feel we could climb Mt. Everest, if only etc... However we are not confronted here simply by what is generally called a high or a low. Both states are most uncomfortable and almost seem to threaten our sanity. How bad it gets depends on how unstable we are temperamentally and on how much experience we have of our inward being. All the same, we will never be asked to put up with more than we can handle. Also, if we neglect to handle it and give in to it to a degree, in the case of the lethargy, or act it out to an extent, in the case of the tension, then we get another opportunity another time, we can count on that. All the same, the most opportune time for cooperation with the necessity of gender is now.

This might be a good time for calling to mind once again how whatever comes our way in terms of elemental reality, such as gender, cannot draw our attention directly while we are still modern. This is why we make contact here with either tension or lethargy. The human heart, to the extent of its modernity, has become accustomed for a while, if only because we were born into the modern world, to acting out its inherited liberty either on the side of mortality or with respect to immortality. Putting it this way might sum it up for us sufficiently for the moment. On account of something that was achieved two-thousand years ago, we are, aboriginally, dual in nature until we discover a way of unifying those two sides – as we rely on that achievement. Much of what has been laid down in history, as record and tradition, for the benefit of our salu-tary reflection, demonstrates this one-sided struggle of human beings to realize themselves in a one-sided fashion in accordance with ego and self, which in themselves are, in point, fictions construed by us in fear and trembling as we notice that we are not really one. Ego and self then seem to assure a degree of permanence, each for itself, and from this springs much of our so-called culture and civilization. Since we identify with our ego and/or our self, we do not take kindly to being reminded of our pre-dicament. Elementary reality reminds us. Gender necessarily reminds us. Anyone who comes along and says: "I am the one, believe in me, love me, follow me," and if we can point him or her out to one another, then he is evidently not the true one within us. Also remember that ego, in the presence of the true one within, causes us to experience horror and to become furious while self, in the presence of the true one, causes us to be cowardly and ashamed.

So much for the general wisdom that helps us come to grips with the reason for viewing both the tension and the lethargy that are due to gender-substance equally as doors through which we can enter into the good that is evidently ready for us. The more we understand this, the easier it will be for us to avoid any confusion with sex when the time comes.[1]

Now one is tempted to say that whenever our ego or our self is threatened, simply seek the truth. Seek the truth in person. However who knows the truth? Mind you, that is precisely why we do well to search for the truth, precisely because it is neither outside nor inside us but within us. Nor do we know what it is. If we look for a needle, even in a haystack, we at least know what we are looking

---

[1] Our chosen topic does not allow us to discuss the *procreative urge* because it is not an *elemental or generic drive* but an erotic urge. Love itself is what urges us – and how readily is that love not falsified! We have tried to explain the difference between the so-called sex drive and the procreative urge elsewhere. Enough said here, that the procreative urge does not announce itself as tension or lethargy; it is not a reactive phenomenon but a way to be. Sexually is how we <u>react</u> to the generic drive. The sex-drive is merely an unfortunate reactive falsification of the generic drive and leads to dissipation, not growth; to squandering, not gathering.

for. We know what a needle looks like and when we come upon it in that haystack we will recognize it and shout: Hurray! I have found it. Not so with the truth. We do not know what it looks like. So how can we, in all sincerity, advise someone to search for he truth? Those who come upon the name Jesus of Nazareth in the Hebrew Gospels, and he says there: "I am the truth, I am the life and the resurrection," and so on, they will still ask: "Where is he?" He is within you, we tell them, in your very human-natural heart, and perhaps if we ourselves know that with the certainty of experience and practical conviction, some of them, or only one maybe, will suddenly be touched by the truth, but there is no guarantee. Evangelists forever travel to far-away places to broadcast a creed, based not on any experience of the truth but on who knows what, and perhaps the creed will catch on here and there, and that may be better than nothing, however it does not amount to personal knowledge of the personal truth, does it.

All the same, when elemental gender rises in us, the first time we are liable to be subjected to the experience of our life. Which is not to say that we have not, until then, grown morally and ethically. On the basis of knowing what is good and actually doing good we can possibly realize ourselves in satisfactory fashion, depending of course on who we are and what we amount to from birth. It is a mistake to suppose that we are all cut out for the truth in person and for a personal experience of it. While we differentiate between the children of wisdom and those who are not children of wisdom, we do not reject anyone, basically because we know that no one is rejected. We sorrow when we see how many reject the truth.

So we try to keep in mind the manifold appeal of the truth. At the same time we feel content that our rather specialised study of the human-natural heart from a psychic point of view contributes to the welfare of our community.

*

One way to search for the truth then, at any time, is to abstract from all our experience whatever does not pertain to our present being. Again, this is easily said. To be or not to be, says Hamlet, which seems to suggest to us that he has the choice and that he is able to tell the one from the other, being from non-being, in the first place. Then, he says, he might have the choice either to suffer or else to oppose afflictions. Then he slips into a state of 'lethargy', as we might call it, to make a case for our argument, in that he inclines to the attractions of sleep and dream. Conscience, with respect to a puzzling afterlife, seems to be preventing him from making a choice at all, for he ends up neither suffering nor opposing, neither properly being nor not being. So the modern tragedy of mutually negating opposites eventually claims him as another victim. Macbeth opposed and arrived at a similar modern-tragic end – in terms of the tension that caused him to commit murder. The genius of Shakespeare, like no playwright before or after him, documented this modern 'hang-up', which reveals to us, in our own lives, the need to come to terms, as soon as possible once we are adults, with the elementary aspect of our human nature – as it arises betimes psychically in our human-natural heart.

The elemental tension and the elemental lethargy are psychic. All that pertains to them is psychic and therefore phenomenal. It is what we have to go on, if we want to make headway, in the direction of that which will supply us with the unifying principle, with the one thing that will not divide into left and right, into up and down, into far and near and leave us stranded between the two, neither able to choose nor not to choose.

Those who have been vouchsafed an experience of the unifying principle, out of the blue as it were, or 'from above', will not say to us: You too must wait until this 'happens' to you, but they will share their knowledge, understanding and wisdom with us, so that we will be able to increase the likelihood of ourselves being enlightened. So that is why we do well to turn to those who have been chosen to know, so that we too will know. Wisdom is given to a few, so that they will make it available to several and to many.

One of the central teachings we will have to take on board is that the unifying and healing principle resides within us, from where it more or less agitates in order to be known. What we initially come across, from within us, therefore, is the evidence of our rejection of it. Even those who are chosen are initially assailed by seemingly endless challenges and difficulties until they manage to identify the reason and purpose of them, and this will then allow them to make sense of their afflictions. Wisdom may come to us from without or from within. We may gain it from within or from without. Even at this moment I am beset with lethargy. What I know from my own experience in the past is that this is simply a case of the elemental truth seeking recognition within me and eager for expression in cooperation with me. I will therefore not 'oppose' this lethargy. I will see through it and identify 'within' it the agitating reality that wishes to reveal itself to me as new. It suffices that I understand that all that I feel and sense as sluggish and dull, for instance, is but a passing fancy, a phenomenon of no account, a psychic fluctuation, the purpose of which is nothing but to alert me to new life on the way in my direction and perfectly accessible to me if I do not allow myself to be swayed in any way. At the same time I know that at any moment the diametrically opposite phenomenon may assail me, namely an uncommon excitement of so-called good spirits, really high spirits, which usually, more likely than not if I indulge them (or myself (my self) in them) mislead me into areas of conflict and desperation.

So I do have the opportunity here to describe this action germane to my creative human heart, specifically as it allows me to take intelligent advantage of this psychic indication, this lethargy, in the interest of what I may call new life, in general of, more specifically, evolutionary growth. The reader may notice how my progress is not modern, in that I do not apply myself in terms of mind alone, or of body alone. I do not employ conceptual thought at the expense of feeling or sense-experience to the detriment of judgment, but I proceed and progress in the name of the one who is known to me, for example, as the truth.

This might be the best time now for me to plan ahead a little, in that I propose to pay some contemporary attention not only to the effectiveness of the truth but also to those other, aforementioned manifestations of merciful good spirit, namely the light, the way, the life and the word. Each time we will be saying the same but in a slightly different guise and this will have two more or less identifiable results, namely to alert us to the great wealth of available life from within us and at the same time it will open our eyes somewhat, hopefully, to the various modern distortions and misrepresentations of those five realities – not, I might add, so that we will criticize but so that we will learn to appreciate.

When we speak of the wealth of new life from within us we surely do not refer to anything that remains within us but rather to that which manifests itself outwardly, again in cooperation with our human-naturally creative efforts and ambitions. We seek to make our inward life manifest so that we and those of our community will have access to it outwardly. That, metaphorically speaking, is, after all, the overarching purpose of our human heart. We may think of our organic heart as the winepress from which flows the wine that nourishes both us and others. Caught up in our modern presumptions, by comparison now, we will always attempt to differentiate first between two opposites so that we can then proceed to still our agitation about this 'discovery' by inventing something that will eventually, if we just keep going at it energetically enough and for long enough, turn into 'the unified field', or the language from which all languages originally sprang, or the medication that will 'cure' us of everything so that we may exist forever. Whatever we will choose to call it, the accent will always be on the prestige that the discovery will hopefully earn us and, more importantly, on the *mighty* uses we will be able to make of what we come up with.

The two opposites, however, are not how we would see them through modern eyes. Rather they reveal themselves to us first one, then the other, then the one again, so that we might avail ourselves of what is signalled by them. The task is personal, by definition, not corporate. I have chosen to speak of lethargy and tension. It would be quite silly now to try to found something like a school of thought on the corporate adoption of lethargy and tension as 'the' two sides of the reality we intend to understand. They are, after all, no such thing. Strictly speaking, they are not two of anything. In no way can we contemplate them simultaneously; nor should we attempt to do so. Depending on our make-up and predisposition at a given time and place, we might choose to understand our own forward-striving creativity in a similar fashion or we might proceed quite otherwise. Creative work is tied safely and securely to our human individuality. Any attempt at 'extraterrestrial' unification is out of the question, to put it mildly. There are so many different ways of saying this. The fact that we experience either tension or lethargy testifies to the duality of our organic make-up, to the 'twoness' of what we begin with when we apply ourselves, not to some spooky reality outside or inside ourselves. The 'twoness' itself is not revealed to us by effective good spirit but 'one at a time' so that we might return to good spirit. Originally we were one, we were born one. All sorts of things went wrong. We want to be one again. Happily this is possible for us. It was impossible for the ancients because for them the two incommensurables did not exist. They were neither one *nor* two. Due to the achievement of one man it has become possible for us.

We are ever so grateful. We show our gratitude by making use of what has been made available to us.

*

What I mean when I say that we are one, or whole, that is not the same as being born perfect. This we have to understand before we can come to grips, rationally, with what it means that our human-natural heart, viewed in itself, although psychically compromised from the day we are born on account of neutral environmental influences, nonetheless is capable of purity and chastity, which, when addressed from without, first parentally and then masterfully, develops obediently and then evolves as good habit. Good influence tends to keep us on the side of growth; of development and evolution, however we must cooperate. Bad influence tends to divert us from growth. Both in the case of good and of bad influence do psychic phenomena occur in us. Viewed rationally, psychic phenomena are the heart's protection-mechanisms. They are neither bad nor good. We have to take especial care here so that we understand this properly. For one thing, we are comforted by psyche. For another, we are informed by it. That is the initial purpose of psychic phenomena, so that we are not destroyed by good or bad influence. If it sounds strange that we might be destroyed even by good influence, we need only call to mind that any influence cannot but come upon comparative inertia in ourselves, which is quite simply a reluctance to change. What a blessing therefore, that this inertia should be drawn to our attention – or to the attention of those who are responsible for us while we are children!

So we are comforted and informed whether the influence is good or bad – to the extent of our unavoidable reaction to the influence, of course. (Modern art and science?)

The comfort is bodily, the information is mental. We do not have to judge, at this stage; to distinguish between bad and good. All psyche comforts and informs. Keep in mind that we are not, from birth, separately bodily or mental, but physical. Neither, therefore, are we separately comforted or informed, but both. One might speak of comfortable information or of informative comfort, it would amount to the same.

The question arises now: What causes things to go wrong? And they do go wrong, periodically, don't they. Why are we liable, suddenly, to indulge ourselves in sensual comfort quite separately from intelligent information that initially came along with it? The comfort should not even be noticeable to us as such. Or how does it come that the informative aspect of psychic phenomena intrigues us separately from the comfort, when such information, too, should be innate, like the comfort? In other words, how does it come that suddenly we are modern? As before, we continue to be under both good and bad influence, but now we seem to have lost track of the original purpose of psychic phenomena. Are they not to protect us from deterioration and to help us back to continued growth, which is to say to further development and evolution? Have we lost the plot, all of a sudden?

Well, it can happen. After all we are not only born physically intact and at liberty from fatality and from the fear of fatality, but we also carry within us some memory of our ancient incarceration. From the point of view of

21

our personal, mature awareness of ourselves as human beings, we are saved and at liberty inasmuch as we can never be utterly annihilated. However, while the road to perfection and freedom lies open to us, we are nonetheless meanwhile at liberty to recall the time when human beings struggled under the yoke of inescapable death. This is not a memory of ourselves but more or less a memory of how times *must have been* prior to our liberation. Not only is this a memory, but it is accidental. We do actually mean that it is accidental when we call it *a* memory.

This memory is liable to rise in us; we do not bring it on. We can however do something to make it less likely that it will come upon us. And here, as is usually the case when we want to rid ourselves of something detrimental, we do not succeed by trying to suppress it but by replacing it with 'the good version'. In our present case therefore, we may put it this way: Any ancient memory, which is bound to disturb us and to mislead to all sorts of errors and horrors, can be replaced by us as soon as possible when we instead remember – actively and creatively remember – that in truth we are 'saved'. We are at liberty to become free.

We are quite right to call this a creative remembering because we do , after all, overcome by this act something thoroughly detrimental and – and – we gain thereby, creatively, what we can justifiably call *the essential impulse for evolutionary growth.*

We can correctly identify at this stage our unwillingness to remember creatively as the cause of our endlessly modern development and of our hankering for more and more development and the pride we take in being developed countries and our pseudo-virtuous attempts to develop countries we describe, self-justifiably, as underdeveloped – and consequently we never really evolve. We do not mature and ripen and bear fruit. The so-called fruits of mere development are all counterproductive and determined to be lost. The proper consequences of development, however, are evolutionary changes and evolutionary results which all amount to the various aspects of eternal life on earth.

It is up to us therefore to acquaint ourselves as thoroughly as possible with creative memory – with what it amounts to and with where it leads.

*

As moderns we are stuck with comfort that has gone miserable and bad and with information that is trivial and extinct, and from those twin standpoints we pit ourselves against the ancient memories, forever hopeful of suppressing them so as to safeguard our liberty, while ignorant of true freedom. Our psyche threatens to tear us apart. Mere comfort superdevelops to the point of obesity and pornography while mere information practically forces us to measure everything in sight and superdevelops to the point of total cellular dissolution. As moderns we never get away from our ancient memories because we try to suppress them. As a consequence we become involved in them. Our evolution cannot commence. The greater the superdevelopment, the less likely is our evolution. However all the same our eventual evolution is an iron necessity. We will never be forgotten by the spirit who creates us for the purpose of evolution. While we insist on non-cooperation we make ourselves and one another miserable.

*

The ancient memories occur to us as an overpowering misery. Happily, due to our inborn liberty, we cannot actually take up with them. We cannot confront them or deal with them. In short we do not actually remember anything in particular, we are only made aware – forced to become aware – of ourselves as tragic misfits who are forever implicated in our own death-wish – which is of course meaningless. What I mean by 'death-wish' is the unavoidable reaction to superabundance and superdevelopment. In short, the liberty that, by definition, is opportunity for freedom, turns into a curse. The fact that we cannot come to terms with the ancient memories that disturb our sleep and undermine our daylight hours means that they turn into a mystical mist as we turn towards them.

The ancient memories have become something of a preoccupation for us at present. We do well to keep in mind meanwhile that creative memory of truth in person commences – or recommences – our evolution, so that we move away from that debilitating shadow on our soul and invest in maturity.

There is, however, such a thing as a refractory preoccupation with the misery that accompanies persistent development when evolution should logically begin. It is a stiff-necked unwillingness to be informed and comforted from without when these two press into us as one. The name I have given to this persistent irrationality in the face of available physical rationality is mysticism.

I hasten to distinguish once again between mysticism and mystical knowledge. When someone makes a career out of this perfectly logical pursuit of mystical knowledge as though it might be an end in itself rather than yet another means towards human maturity, we call him a mystic and expect from him mysticism, but nothing that lives or supports life. The fact that he does not even help us to survive causes us to wonder why he bothers. It is decidedly a hopeless endeavour, that we should pit ourselves against the results of our neglect rather than making up for our negligence. Comfort and information as separate, signal for us our available liberty to pursue freedom. We mistake our liberty for freedom itself and the ancient memories move in. We are faced with a miserable existence. We claw at comfort to make it stay and we grasp at information until it turns massive. Now and again some glimmer of the truth, the light, the way, the life or the word brings us to our senses for a moment, in case we should change course. These very glimmers the mystic mistakes for something he has created; against all odds, in the most stiff-necked pursuit imaginable, he spins a cocoon of supernatural personality. A new religion is liable to develop. Several have become quite lucrative in our time.

*

We must let it be enough for us that our human existence is mysterious without trying to make a mystery out of it. No doubt our super-developmental preoccupations lead us astray. This is understandable, because human evolution is a major step forward for us and can even threaten us as something like the last and final act beyond which we cannot imagine what comes next. Not until we set out upon our evolution do we distinctly realize then that this is not a stage, like development, but rather that towards which we develop and into which we enter, with a shout of jubilation and with a sigh of relief. Certainly it may be our task thereafter to document the journey for others, but this task will not be so much exploratory now, as it must always be for the developing will or intellect, but rather revelatory, because we take upon ourselves vicariously the trials and afflictions of those who still develop, so as to enact for them, in exemplary fashion, the move towards, and into, evolution. In the meantime, of course, our own evolution proceeds. Gradually, as time passes, we see more clearly where we are, now that we have arrived, and in addition we are able to reveal in greater depth and breadth what it means and what it can mean for a human being to evolve.

While we develop we exist for ourselves. We learn what it means to be a human being rather than a popular individual, a responsible person rather than a selfish thing. We learn to love and become aware of the difference between loving and liking. We learn how to communicate and become aware of the difference between speaking and talking. We become aware of ourselves as members of a community rather than of a society, a club or a crowd. It is quite right that we should exist for ourselves and invest as energetically as possible in our development. A selfish individual does not exist for himself; he rejects others. This is an important difference. When I exist for myself I fully take account of the fact that by being generous, kindly, forgiving etc. towards others, I gain my own advantage. I understand that by holding a grudge or by being dishonest and unjust I harm myself. By comparison, there is such a thing as arrested development, such as when we take it upon ourselves to educate others before we know anything ourselves; when we try to export development as an end in itself rather than as the stage towards evolution. Arrested development can become downright virulent at times when the need for evolutionary measures presses in upon people and painfully draws to their attention their unwillingness to mature.

Indeed, since our openness to evolution counts, it makes little difference whether we stop in our development because of ignorance and laziness or because we try to settle down in it out of fear of the unavoidable goal. Arrested development and super-development are two phenomena therefore that can be summed up as avoidance of evolution. Clearly we should never lose track, at any stage of our development, of the fact that development is towards evolution, even as youth is towards maturity and not a search for eternal youth.

Since we live on earth and not in some imaginary state of being (where we barely tick over), our personal development naturally takes into account what we mean by our economical, political and scientific development, to mention only three. Here too development gets stuck or goes awry if we get caught up in final states of being, such as an ever growing economy, permanent nationality and the scientific knowledge of everything. Instead we do well to look forward, while we develop, to living reflectively within our means in a country that values its friendly disposition towards other countries. With such a goal in mind, we may look forward to an appropriate future instead of getting caught up in absurd projects or steeping in our own juices.

*

1. Psychic life and eternal life:

We make such a thing, nowadays, out of development without having any sensible notion of where we are going, that if we want to say something about development specifically towards evolution we might do well to begin at the beginning. Naturally one can only give a few hints when researching such a huge topic. Certainly there are as many ways to develop as there are human interests and opportunities, so once again I will limit myself to what I mean by the truth, the life, the light, the word and the way. I consider these to be five important universal directions and attractions – one or the other depending on whether we allow ourselves to be led and wait until we are persuaded or else we pick and choose whatever occurs to us to be worth doing.

By the life I mean eternal life, not psychic life, and clearly our development would involve first and foremost an increasingly clear distinction between the two and the choice of the former over the latter. Now this is easily said but not readily done. However unless we have become thoroughly degenerate, we should be able to detect, within ourselves, at least a memory of the life that resides within itself and promises both a satisfaction of the senses and a nourishment of the intellect. We became acquainted somewhat with what we called the 'ancient memory' and its chaos a little while ago, and this present, revealed memory of eternal life is certainly distinguishable by its beauty and peacefulness. If instead we insist on a contin-

28

uation of intellect and sense as separate, the ancient memory will proportionately gain headway and our development will stagnate.

Secondly, once we have noticed both the psychic and the eternal life, we will very likely wish to discover how the latter can be gained, though not at the expense of the former. We know readily enough that we may cause the psychic life; that we may bring it about. We assume there is a direct causal relationship between what we do, how we behave, on one side and the quality and duration of our psychic life on the other. We presume to know what makes us happy, what gives us satisfaction and pleasure, and we cling to this while we can. The eternal life meanwhile tends to lie outside our sphere of reference until unhappiness, dissatisfaction and pain begin to burden us because we cannot after all, as it turns out, control the psychic life. Now we entertain the thought of eternal life and hope to come to some arrangement with it while we still cling to the positive aspect of the psychic life. Surely, we suppose, the eternal life is a continuation into a higher sphere of manipulation and mastery of the psychic life. When this proves unworkable, we assume that the pain we experience must somehow relate to the eternal life because with increasing frequency we notice that any attention we pay to eternal life has to pass through a period of suffering. When we antagonize those who mean us ill, we suffer dire consequences and if we suffer willingly we learn not to antagonize them in future. Now we learn that this is still not quite enough. It appears we must not only be positive but actually do positive. At this stage of our development we usually try to find some name for what ails us as we feel pushed to the limit of our tolerance. It occurs to us that we are, after all, not in overall control and we invent a 'higher power', as we think of it, which we may have to bribe, to flatter and to obey in order to sway it in our favour. This takes us to the next stage of our development. We have invented a mighty God who is inscrutable and whose law is insurmountable. If any doubt enters our breast as to the genuineness of this God, we set out to persuade as many others as possible of what we fear. We fear this mighty God and we do our best to make this fear look like something else, because no one likes to be known to be afraid. So we might produce a false reverence or become fanatical. In the meanwhile merciful good spirit continues to influence us. During the last stage of our development, this spirit enters us and draws our attention more thoroughly to the difference between what we invent to please ourselves and what comes our way gratis, mostly during moments of weakness and anxiety. Merciful spirit now moves into the place that had been occupied by the invented God. We are now more than willing to draw on the various types of input from this spirit. We learn that this spirit cannot be coerced, caused or bribed but that there are various kinds of being and behaviour that render us acceptable (able to accept). We distinguish between what is up to us and what we must leave up to merciful good spirit. What is up to us now moves into first place and our psychic life move into second place, where we recognize it for what it is and for what it is not. Just like that we continue until the commencement of our evolution. Thereafter eternal life is ours and we turn away from our developmental cautions and designs so as to be able to turn entirely towards the wellbeing and welfare of others in our community. Eternal life is itself creative and we prepare ourselves for this creativity on a daily basis.

a. What lies ahead for a developing human being?

How wonderful if the evolution of human beings were to begin with their adulthood! The early years, up to adulthood, would then be dedicated to development. Mankind itself has not evolved to that stage however, so how can we expect that an individual human being of the twenty-first century would automatically enter upon eternal life between the years of, say, eighteen and twenty-four, or thereabouts? A few forerunners have appeared however, and we depend upon them to enlighten us about what is on the way.

What would help immensely from the start is any amount of experience that may be narrated by those who are in the know – I mean experience both of the transition from psychic life to eternal life and of eternal life itself. Eternal life in our time may come upon a hapless human being as quite a shock, mainly because the language necessary for communicating this experience is not readily available to anyone. It is certainly not available to your average parent or schoolteacher – not to mention the purveyors of 'higher education'. So this would surely rate high as an important task for those few who have lived through this transition and must surely be eager to translate what has happened to them, for others.

For example, if I say that I have no wish to think myself into the condition of an individual, especially if that individual has no intention to reflect upon his predicament, will I be understood by anyone? Or if I say that the cultivation of happiness is a cause of bad health, or that the barrage of categories in the extinct sciences is what stupefies the youth of today – I wonder how that would go down. Let's face it, it lies there on the page like a boulder that has rolled onto a meadow. At the same time, those are true statements and entirely open for discussion – if anyone can be found to discuss them.

So my point is, that evolution here and now, like eternal life here and now, is not readily relatable to our physical existence on earth in the twenty-first century. In addition to this, human development in general has long ago passed the mark where it really should have flowed like a tributary into the sea of evolution. Development has become super-development – and is no longer relevant for any organic transition into the life that comes our way spontaneously and lies ready for us to welcome it the moment we arrive at that distinct realization of ourselves as beings both mortal and immortal, at liberty to construct our freedom. In the end it may well turn out to be easier for so-called underdeveloped countries to enter upon their evolution than for those who are superdeveloped and measure their development in terms of psychic phenomena as things in themselves.

The consensus of the civilized populations seems to centre on the psychic life under the law. The mystery of our rational human existence has in part been explained away and what is left masquerades as a mathematical magic alongside a popular romanticism. A new-born child opens its eyes onto a world that is divided against itself and the infant wisdom in vain seeks counterpoise and complement. Voters dutifully march to the ballot box with not a notion in the world as to the crucial and time-honouring difference between a nation-state and a country; between society and community, between policies and values – in short, between psyche and soul.

Youthful development towards maturity cannot succeed if maturity is not viewed and understood by parental adults as spiritually and carnally whole. Unless the young are encouraged to become aware, and helped to remain aware, of their inborn liberty, they will neither expect nor demand the required expansion and discipline required for mature thinking and feeling. We are not born free, but we are born at liberty – to sink or to learn to swim. This is the liberty at the centre of modern existence. It is the reason for our ability to view ourselves as noble beings – and due to our inescapable liberty, if we try to ignore or misrepresent it, we experience all the tensions and anxieties of the modern, psychic life.

*

b. Direction or attraction as developmental dynamics:

During our development we may choose to push ahead to the best of our ability, keeping the goal in mind and making efficient use of materials at our disposal, or we may wait for things to happen, for events to take shape, and then we deal with them and find our way. Some prefer one to the other. What counts is that we learn as early as possible – and teach as soon as appropriate, if we are parents or teachers – that this duality exists and, impossible as it must remain to find a common denominator for them – such as, for example, calling them two approaches or two attitudes – that we encourage both, whichever comes to the fore, and disparage neither.

Open-mindedness is called for with respect to a young person's being and doing – and also, of course, if we suppose we are in a position to advise a young country. There is no substitute for thoroughly getting to know someone before we offer advice, that should go without saying. Youth must be allowed to demonstrate its preferences. This is the same as saying that a young being needs time to discover and come to suitable terms with the liberty towards freedom within its natural being. Only then can one know how best to raise someone towards evolutionary maturity.

It will help us in our parental endeavours if we remain aware of direction and attraction as equally viable during development. And always we are given the lead by the being for which we have decided to assume responsibility. What is required at the moment may be a hand up or a kindly word, a new challenge or reassurance. A useful comparison might be the one between being and doing. Learning how to be, at a given time, might be as crucial during development as learning how to do. Both action and passion are called for at different times, at different stages of development. If we keep in mind the fundamental difference between attraction and direction we will not get bogged down in contradictions which, by the way, are not dualities. So for example it would be quite wrong to insist that someone should choose between good and bad, between right and wrong, true and false. That is another issue altogether and barely plays into the developmental growth as such. We limit ourselves in the present work to the realm of psychology, which is to say to the discovery of the human soul in the jungle of psychic aims and predispositions.

We also differentiate between how someone develops and the particular stage of development at which he finds himself. Attraction and direction pertain to the former and can guide us if we want to support and encourage from the point of view of evolution. Once we have set out upon our evolutionary growth, we have only the one teacher, within us, who shows us and draws our attention to the different kinds of development and to the various features of it in those who are to be helped by us.

On the practical level, an individual may be attracted to charitable work, to helping where he feels help is needed. In such a case he should not be persuaded or dissuaded but the nature of charity can be elucidated for him and the role it plays in terms of personal satisfaction, while the continued attraction of the subject is not touched upon. Or if a country seems to be developing in the direction of increased agriculture, those who are in the know do well to allow it to discover in its own time and by its own lights what works and what does not work. We all learn best by our mistakes. It is quite wrong to destroy a country's poppy crop if cocaine is illegally marketed and leads to drug addiction. Let the market for it be regulated and then the farmers will learn to grow something else. If the fields of poppies, which represent the farmer's industry, are destroyed, this defeats the human being and he comes up with nothing better. Or if the Maasai lion hunter, who traditionally protects the herds, is punished for decimating the lion population that is required for the lucrative tourism, his spirit is defeated and he will not come up with the courage for undertaking some other useful activity, the likes of which can be intelligently presented to him, so that he will be attracted by some personal activity that appeals to him or inwardly directed towards some other communal service that suits him.

So we can see how developmental strategies must be arranged from without by those who evolve, however the spirit of the developing being must be honoured. Attraction and direction are not strategies but helpful ways of how we can imagine how beings develop.

*

Psychic truth and eternal truth:

Truth, for the psychic mind, which is to say for the mind on its own, is simply what can be shown to exist. Show us clearly what you mean and we will listen to you. Then there is the inward human realm of truth in which all that is, is represented in some shape or form and available to faith and knowledge. No two definitions could be further apart – in fact so far apart as not be in sight of each other. The physical truth, let us call it, which is perceived by body and mind as one, does not in the beginning have an outside shell, as it were. If we want to know how beings are connected or how they know of one another, we have to be wise. This wisdom is a unique faculty. Little children, as we know, are wise because their organ of physical truth-perception has not yet been spoiled or stretched beyond recognition on the rack of materialism or spiritualism. There is no reason I can think of at the moment why the wisdom of children should not develop gradually and turn into the wisdom of the man or the woman. If by wisdom we mean knowledge of the truth, which is what I myself mean by wisdom at the moment, then the only thing that radically changes from childhood to mature adulthood is the perception of world, which understandably becomes less like a dream and more three-dimensional.

Truth implies connection and relation of being. Here we have the equivalent of attraction and direction again. Connection of being means that a few, several or many are in touch and know themselves to be in touch and they understand this as the guarantee of eternal life. You notice that there is no mention of 'all' or of 'everything' being in touch but of a few, several or many. This is important, even crucial. Neither do I say a few human beings, several horses, many trees. The truth is of beings. In addition to connection we also know of the relation of beings. This takes care of change, inasmuch as relation implies connection again. Finally then we can sum up by saying that truth implies connection and relation of beings.

During the course of this paragraph I have progressed from being to beings. This is as it should be, because truth is always personal. What I have written here could not have been written by anyone else. Also, I could not have written it at any other time. Thirdly, the fact that it was given to me to write this in cooperation with creative spirit and that I did not figure it out intellectually or concoct it emotionally allows me to say that the truth is creative spirit. By saying so, I express my gratitude.

Due to the fact that I have come to terms with the live truth in a way, I am now in a position to say something helpful about the psychic truth – which has nothing whatsoever to do with the connection and the relation of being and beings but with a degree of fit of appearance with substance. If there is any degree of fit at all, we say that something might be true and if there is a large degree of fit we say that something is probably true or very true. The simple truth of the connection and relation of beings remains hidden from our psyche and is only revealed to our soul.

Such a rational description of psychic truth cannot possibly be taken on board by us if we are under the influence of psyche and while our soul is hidden from us. It is a description that makes sense to us while we are in the possession of our soul. Knowing and understanding as much about psychic truth helps us to be tolerant of those who swear by 'their' psyche and who will go to any length to argue and fight and kill about their own version of psychic truth as though it were 'the truth'. In the meantime we are allowed to understand that this so-called truth is not for us to dispute or to criticize or to judge. However since we know that substance, i.e. humanity, is involved in such cases and at such times, we may be able to do some good – not by arguing, contradicting or in any way trying to prove to the one who is under the influence of psyche that he is under the influence of psyche but by being and behaving truthfully. We are truthful while we know and believe in the personal truth and we behave truthfully if we attend, while we behave, to our connection and relation with a few, several or many beings. – Practice turns a complicated sounding instruction into good habit.

While we are in the possession of our soul it may occur to us to protect ourselves against psychic influence. This is perfectly understandable. While we exist in cooperation with our soul, our existence is orderly and peaceful. Psychic behaviour in our vicinity is bound to appear as disorder and discord and this frightens us, we shrink from it, because we literally fear – not for our soul, even though we may suppose that this is the cause of our fear, but for that sense of peace and orderliness. However we make a simple mistake. The truth of the matter is that we are in the possession of our soul while we cooperate with it truthfully not while we cling to attributes such as peace and an orderly existence. So we are well advised patiently to suffer the discord and the disorder. This is something we do; more, it is something we do well to decide to do as soon as we fear for our peace and orderliness. And then it would be just a bit silly of us to suppose that 'these things are sent to try us', because let's face it, while we think and feel like that, we are still labouring under the illusion that we might, if we are good little boys and girls, exist forever in peace and quiet and in the possession of our soul if we avoid trouble and just mind our own business, whatever that is. Technically however we are hopeful of being left in the possession not of our soul but of our psyche.

It is in this particular lazy hope that we enter upon our psychic existence, so that we eventually become a scandal upon the earth, a trial to our fellow man and a disappointment to god. Instead of continuing to thrive in community with our fellow man, we barricade ourselves behind civic obedience, within the ideal of a lawful and orderly society and we create a humanist morality and ethic so that our continued psychic existence shall at least remain comparatively bearable. We pride ourselves on civilized behaviour which is, in reality, yet another insurance policy against loss of ultimately unsustainable peace and orderliness.

Psychic light and eternal light:

Light implies clarity. The eternal light shines on us both night and day. Of course we do not see the light itself, but we know that it shines when we know and understand the truth.

We distinguish between the knowledge that is based on faith and the knowledge based on evidence from sense data. If we begin with faith, our senses are true and come up with knowledge. If we begin with sense data our knowledge is always unstable and questionable.

What the eternal light shines upon is available to us inasmuch as we believe so that we may see. The psychic light allows us to see so that we may believe or not believe, as we see fit. The fit has to be between what we look at and whatever psychic knowledge we have accumulated so far.

Eternal believing, by comparison, highlights for us what is worth seeing and casts in shadow what would be detrimental for us to see.

According to the modern way of thinking, imagining and knowing, we begin with sense data and call the result objective knowledge. We set out to see what there is and we suppose that what is 'there', if clearly seen, is real and true. If we are unclear about what it is we see there, we look for more evidence. Of course the entire modern existence depends on such sense appreciation even as it presumes the fact of genuine appearance. The psychic light shines on things and causes them or allows them to appear. It causes them or allows them to appear depending on whether our will or our intellect is more involved. Whichever is the case, what appears is things, not beings. Everything we see, hear, touch or feel in the modern fashion is a thing or a combination of things, which implies that the appearance and that which appears do not match. Sometimes we find this quite upsetting, however after a time it is what we expect and we make allowances for it. At other times we lie to ourselves.

The thing-based reality excludes us. We behave as though what we were looking at and seeing really had nothing to do with us and we take pride in having discovered something that is not faulty like ourselves. This works best if we succeed in lying to ourselves about the fact that the thing we know, and its appearance that we see, do not match.

*

Eternal light is what brings about the function of the human eye. If there were no eternal light we would not be able to see. Now that we are able to see we are at liberty to choose between the psychic and the eternal light. I can think of only one reason why we would ever choose to see by the psychic light, and that is *infantile regression*. If, as children, we are not raised and if we are left to our devices and are perhaps right from the start exposed solely to the psychic light, we drift away, as it were, from our inborn ability to perceive by the eternal light that always shines upon us. Our eyesight dims and from the point of view of the eternal light we become blind. Our eye is then no longer stimulated to perceive the light that stems equally from within and from without us and we depend on things to stimulate us. Then, gradually, we get into the habit of differentiating between objective and subjective reality, between what we can point at and our reactions to ideas, and also between one another's individual points of view as the sole criteria of judgment. Not that the eternal light no longer shines on us but that we create various barriers between it and us which, perversely, we then identify as the causes of our uncertainty, of our insecurity and of various mental perturbations. We do not go so far as to blame our hands that we hold before our eyes for our blindness but we do, in our modern fashion, try to achieve certainty, security and peace of mind by means of psychic light.

This, needless to say, surely, is wrong from the start.

The unfortunate condition of infantile regression can stay with us for the rest of our days on earth. If at any time, during our adult years, it should occurs to us that it might conceivably be up to us actually to see through the film we have miscreated for ourselves, we have to start by acquainting ourselves with how this condition of infantile regression has, in our particular and individual case, managed to present itself. In other words, once we are dissatisfied with not being able to see, it is within the specific phenomenon of our dissatisfaction that we have to search for the hindrances to the eternal light that we are putting up, because that is where they are being signposted. To the extent that we are content with the thing-consciousness and with the arbitrary conscience of the modern tradition we are not very likely to try to come to terms with what anyone means who tells us about the difference between the psychic and the eternal light.

How fortunate if in our youth it is given to us to challenge the psychic light that has been presented to us as the basis for rational knowledge. There seem to me to be more and more young people in the world who are not merely upset with the older generation because that is, and has been for so long, par for the course, but they seem to sense that something essential within themselves is not being addressed even by the most well-meaning advocates of the status quo. One explanation that occurs to me is that the eternal light is shining with increasing intensity upon them both from within and from without. What most vividly suggests itself to them is how they in their particular individuality have been wronged and are still being wronged. Since they are not yet adults, they do not have to concern themselves about any complicity. And what they would be advised to get over as soon as possible is any accusation and blame they feel inclined to levy. Let them be assured that there is nothing to be gained in that direction. Parents and teachers may well be to blame inasmuch as they have catered to the traditional and social malaise, however the young person hasn't the time for blaming them because he (or she) is much too busy ascertaining what has gone wrong and making up for it.

The most elementary item that will not have been addressed is the unique individuality of the young person. As a matter of fact, during the early years of infantile regression any genuine individuality, any wish or drive to be as no one else can be or ever could be, will have been thwarted, so that with the greatest candour we can speak, to this young person, of a build-up of negativity in him- or herself. Also we must let it be known that the most toxic negativity is resentment. It is a resentment of which the young person does not become aware until a glimmer of eternal light has broken into his awareness of himself. Now, we must know, he will first be resentful, and only then might he choose to inspect that resentment for a way out of it. Any psychic light he lets shine on this resentment aggravates it and before long he is finding fault left and right. The worst that can happen to him now is that he indulges in criticism. As soon as we – we mature adults – notice this, let us be aware of it as yet another symptom of infantile regression, which we, from the outside, cannot help him with unless we cleverly steer him towards a recognition of it as a means towards automatic, authentic regeneration. This regeneration will be automatic as soon as we, who want to help, learn to encounter his resentment or his criticism as a cry for help from his soul. We in our own soul hear this cry and respond to it compassionately. The healing-influence will be spontaneous, of course, not mechanical. The regeneration will be authentic in future after the young person has caught wind of what is going on during a case of automatic regeneration and as a consequence he turns away from resentment and criticism, either as soon as he notices how it crops up in him or even better, as he feels that it might crop up.

Every young person who is being subjected to – or objects to – eternal light will be resenting something else and will be resentful of something else. What is at stake after all is his (or her) individuality, which by definition is unique. He will not do himself a favour by teeming up with others on a joint venture of criticism or resentment. It stands to reason that it will be proportionately that much more difficult for him to bring himself around to looking to his true advantage.

*

The psychic word and the eternal word:

This difference can perhaps best be highlighted by comparing what we do when we talk with what we do when we speak. We can say the first thing that occurs to us or we can reflect on it before we speak. We can have a chat about anything under the sun for the sheer enjoyment of it. Or we give a speech in some public forum and we have carefully taken into consideration why we are about to do this and who is likely to be listening to what we say.

When we write creatively, several other factors come into play. Before I sat down to put pen to paper today, I put myself properly in touch with myself. As a consequence I was able to continue where I had left off two days ago and I could be sure that nothing would occur to me that was pointless or meaningless in relation to the topic I had set myself. I am, of course, at liberty to make a mess of things but this will not happen while I remain carefully in touch with the true source of language within me.

This true source of language is not on its own the source of true language. What I myself have to bring to this source, so that it will, so to speak, flow, is my own heartfelt desire for the truth. Only in that way can language, as it comes to the fore, be embodied. The word becomes flesh.

Why is it important that 'the word should become flesh'? This is a question only those will feel inclined to ask who have in their personal possession what it takes to give both berth and birth to 'the word', to true speech, to good language. We consider a time of gestation followed by a period of achievement.

Now when we speak of 'the word' we have in mind a mythic entity. We mean, in general, our capacity for utterance, which is both matter and manner of speech. However a capacity, in our head as it were, is not yet a deed or an achievement. A human being must come along to translate 'the word' into words. The intention to speak must be accompanied by our having something to say, otherwise we babble. Then someone else has to come along to translate our babbling. It's best to wait until we have something to say. And we will have something to say as soon as our heart is in the right place. The degenerate heart is never in the right place. The psychic heart babbles. It does not differentiate between meaning and substance, between form and content – in other words, between words and the word. Words come forth as readily as water from a leaking barrel.

Which is not to say that some are not gifted with a ready connection between heart and head. All the same, it is still up to them to honour or abuse that connection. So when we listen carefully we will hear what is going on, what is being achieved and what is amiss – whatever the voice is that utters. Whether it is someone talking to me or someone's poem I am reading or indeed a song sung or a performance on the violin, what I hear is both the degree and the nature of the connection between heart and head, which is the join of capacity and achievement.

What interests us presently, of course, is what, specifically we can do to bring the human heart, primarily ours but then also that of someone else, around to worthwhile achievement. There is liable to be babbling, which is mere noise but at the opposite extreme there is also shrieking and we do well to draw both into account. Between babbling and shrieking we may come across a myriad variations of disconnect between heart and head.

*

Now ancient memories may inform us of a time when heart and head were not yet separate and could therefore not be creatively joined. Since it is the join that counts and not the lack of distinguishable difference, we rightly shy away and stay clear of such ancient memories from inside (not within) ourselves. What we are bound to come across plentifully from outside ourselves primarily and secondarily from inside is the lie that head and heart are not distinct and that anyone who says that they are is lying. The tendency of the times and the spirit of the age however dictate everywhere that head and heart should be joined. The resulting pressure does not allow itself to be taken lightly. Two millennia of anxious productivity testify to he fact. So what is up to us, for but one example, is that in terms of he word too, of language and speech, we take seriously what I mean by the psychology of the human-natural heart, so that we will know and understand what is at stake and so that we will learn how to handle and deal creatively with the widespread modern deception.

*

The psychic way and eternal way:

Everything we are about to do, from being to living, persuades us to ask: How shall we go about it? How can it be done well rather than poorly? What would be the best way to spend the forthcoming day? Or our thinking and feeling might centre on such crucial questions as: How shall I love? How does one go about being merciful? How is it wise to deal with anger, with despondency, with one's friends or enemies?

If we look at despondency, which is besetting me at the moment, we might ask? Do I want this feeling, this state of being, to influence my behaviour? Do I want it to affect the way I get on with those around me? Or would it amount to an inconsideration and an unkindliness if I spread this despondency over my immediate environment?

Psyche right away is willing to accommodate me. Be true to your self, it says. Let your self dictate your behaviour.

Originally we do not walk around with such a thing as a self. Rather it crops up at times when we have reacted to some growth stimulant and would make us believe that our reaction – in the present case my despondency – is real and not unreal. As soon as we begin to deal creatively with the accidental psychic result, our self is gone, in a puff of smoke if you like, and that which seemed to be – no longer seems to be.

We notice here how carefully we have to handle this 'self', lest we make it appear real when in truth there is nothing to appear. Even when I say that something disappears, I suggest that it continues to be but is no longer visible. Consider, for example that the composer J.S.Bach has disappeared but he lives on nonetheless, for example in his works which we have learned to appreciate.

Our self, by comparison, has never really lived or existed. It is a mere signal, nothing else. What does it signal? That the power to do good has entered us. Now let us concentrate on that power by doing good. What about the signal? The self? The psychic non-entity? It falls by the wayside as we set out upon the way. We set out upon what I have chosen to call the eternal way.

Along the eternal way we may come upon the devil who says to us: 'You know in your heart of hearts that I am a mere phantom. Shall we talk about it?'

What we may well ask ourselves now is: Has it indeed come to this that we converse with phantoms? So we go on our way.

Next we come upon strange lights in the sky, lights that blink and flash and shimmer wondrously and a fellow walking beside us whispers in our ear: "It is the end of the world! How about that?" Again there is no need for us to respond. We know the eternal light and this is not it. No need to waste words. Or if we feel capable of the eternal word (as previously mentioned in this essay) we might say: "I know the eternal light and this (which you point at) is not it." Then we continue on our way.

The eternal way, while we develop, is ever beset by pitfalls which challenge us so that we may gain greater insight and understanding as we approach maturity. Once we begin to evolve, our works speak for us and we sympathize with those for whom we are responsible: our children, our community or our fellow man in general. We are compassionate by dint of our mature human nature. We take upon ourselves those onsets of self they cannot handle and we turn them into good works for them.

The eternal way, semi-dark, teasing and inviting during our youth, appearing and reappearing in one way or another to encourage us during trial and error, occurs smoothly before us during maturity, however always engaging our mindfulness of those around us, who have a right to depend on us for helpful information and to look to us both for upbringing and adult education.

It is especially the way out of the modern traps that has to be shown to us, since all that is modern prides itself on being in the possession of the last word, when in truth there is no last word. There is the helpful word, the efficient and expedient word, that points the way and finally there is no way that suits everyone at all times – on the way to the eternal way which is constant change. All true ways lead to god and god is *the* way.

*

If we compare this to what I call – entirely for the purpose of comparison – the psychic way, we first of all have to lay aside all ambition for eternal life. The psyche promises 'the everlasting', which is something quite different, besides being a promise that is not realizable. Once the human heart has given itself over to a method, a technique, a program – be it ever so comprehensive – it can no longer grow in wisdom. Anything that takes away from the individual person his or her opportunity for initiative in the realm of development and evolution condemns him (or her) at best to a lifeless satisfaction, at worst to a stupefying despair.

If by psychology we mean knowledge and understanding of the human psyche specifically for the purpose of translating psychic phenomena into operational soul, then we are justified in asking others to entrust us with their inward anxieties and lethargies. Those who know nothing of every mature human being's operational soul, of the heartfelt need we experience to do well and to do good work, are themselves in need to have a few things pointed out to them before they mislead and betray.

* * *

We have looked at five categories of the human-natural heart's activity as it seeks to free itself – or, to put it another way, as we seek true freedom. Of course one may argue: Is it really helpful to speak of our heart as though it were more – or other – than a biological organ? This organ is however inside us, while we are concerned with the reality within us and that is where mythic entities help us out – as focal points, if you like or as areas of affinity.

Also, while it seems quite possible to speak of direct transition from liberty to freedom, as though our inborn liberty were readily identifiable by many of us as potential and capacity, what we most come across in our vicinity is the result of an unwillingness to take that liberty for granted, as an act of faith. So what develops instead is widespread reaction to the unavoidable duality that comes along with that liberty. Indeed there is endless reaction to reaction, as each attempt to prove that reality is not as it is must end in failure, whereupon this failure leads to more reaction, more resistance and more rejection – while more and more nations pride themselves on becoming 'nuclear' and while more and more individuals survive longer and longer.

So it is that particular predicament that we choose to face. The peace of nations is as much of a pipe-dream as the community of individuals. Mature human beings who live in friendly countries, that is what we are after. To that end we strive to identify the various lies we invent to console ourselves for what is really our unwillingness to practice contrition, to search for our inward reality that can be exemplified as outward works.

The lies I mean bind us to our view of ourselves as biological entities and as organisms. There is the lie that we are really animals and in the same boat with other animals struggling for survival. There is the lie that would have us believe that life and survival amount to the same in the end and that eternal life here and now is a bed-time story for children. Add to this the notion of a supernatural God and before long you will find yourself torn to pieces by endless anxieties or stupefied by an infinite variety of stimulants + opiates.

* * * * *

(April 2017)